I0102410

Philippine Masonic
Directory ~ 1918

Also from Westphalia Press

westphaliapress.org

Philippine Masonic Directory

1918

by Chas. M. Colton

WESTPHALIA PRESS
An imprint of Policy Studies Organization

Philippine Masonic Directory ~ 1918
All Rights Reserved © 2014 by Policy Studies Organization

Westphalia Press
An imprint of Policy Studies Organization
1527 New Hampshire Ave., NW
Washington, D.C. 20036
info@ipsonet.org

ISBN-13: 978-1633910294
ISBN-10: 1633910296

Cover design by Taillefer Long at Illuminated Stories:
www.illuminatedstories.com

Daniel Gutierrez-Sandoval, Executive Director
PSO and Westphalia Press

Devin Proctor, Director of Media and Publications
PSO and Westphalia Press

Updated material and comments on this edition
can be found at the Westphalia Press website:
www.westphaliapress.org

PHILIPPINE
MASONIC
DIRECTORY

1918

.

PHILIPPINE MASONIC DIRECTORY

of

Regular and

Recognized Lodges

—————

March 1, 1918

GRAND LODGE F. & A. M. OF THE PHILIPPINE ISLANDS

Organized 1912

OFFICERS

Manuel L. Quezon .... Grand Master
    Residence: 404 Lamayan,
Milton E. Springer......Deputy Grand Master
Rafael Palma..............Senior Grand Warden
Walter R. Macfarlane, Junior Grand Warden
Pascual Lintag................:.........Grand Treasurer
Newton C. Comfort................Grand Secretary
    Residence 128 San Luis
    Phones: 28 and 4306, P. O. Box 990
Joseph F. Bromfield, Senior Grand Lecturer
Teodoro M. Kalaw......Junior Grand Lecturer
George R. Harvey................Grand Chaplain
Bruce S. Wright.....................Grand Orator
Tomas Earnshaw....................Grand Marshal
Elisha Ward Wilbur............Grand Standard
                                    Bearer
Salvador Chofre............Grand Sword Bearer
Felipe Buencamino, Sr., Grand Bible Bearer
Conrado Bénitez............Senior Grand Deacon
Luther B. Bewley..,......Junior Grand Deacon
Ernest J. Westerhouse............,.Senior Grand
                                    Steward
Faustino Aguilar..........Junior Grand Steward
James McC. Bury................Grand Pursuivant
Charles H. W. Aitken..........Grand Organist
Mariano Santos.............................Grand Tiler

ANNUAL COMMUNICATION

January 28, 1918

Meets in Masonic Temple, The Escolta, Manila

1

MANILA LODGE No. 1, F. & A. M.
Manila

OFFICERS

Charles Maxwell Colton...........................Master
      Residence: 410 Lamayan,
      Phones: 2033 and 5115
Harvey Carlquist......................Senior Warden
Harley I. Mozingo.....................Junor Warden
Bruce Edward Ingersoll....................Treasurer
Lowell Emerson Perry.....................Secretary
      Residence: 123 Padre Faura
      Phones: 4828 and 1750 P. O. Box 407
George Garnett Calkins.....................Chaplain
Leonard Arthur Richard Winkel
                          Senior Deacon
Frank Ostrom Maxwell...........Junior Deacon
Albert Kee Welford..............................Marshal
John Colby Howe.................................Organist
Joseph Lane Beach................Senior Steward
George Anderson Thrum......Junior Steward
Emanuel Newman...................................Tiler

STATED COMMUNICATIONS
First Tuesday each month

ANNUAL COMMUNICATION
December 3, 1918

Meets in Masonic Temple, The Escolta, Manila

2

CAVITE LODGE No. 2, F. & A. M.
Cavite

OFFICERS

Francis Kane..Master
P. O. Box 16, Cavite
Harry Johnson Braman..........Senior Warden
Emanuel Valmas......................Junior Warden
Charles Henry William Aitken......Treasurer
Emory Theodore Ozabal....................Secretary
P. O. Box 16, Cavite
Jesse Munroe Cunningham................Chaplain
Henry Elijah Smith...................Senior Deacon
George William Wilson............Junior Deacon
George Templeton Crosby.................Marshal
Henry Edward McCann........Senior Steward
Thomas Bastain Terkildsen....Junior Steward
Max Frederick Bathke............................Tiler

STATED COMMUNICATIONS
Second Monday each month

ANNUAL COMMUNICATION
December 9, 1918

Meets Masonic Hall. Cavite
3

CORREGIDOR LODGE No. 3, F. & A. M.—Manila

OFFICERS

Wade Clarence West..............................Master
     Residence 602 Tennessee
     Office Bureau of Public Works
     Phone: 870 and 4462
Walter John Grodske............Senior Warden
Hugh Merril Johnston............Junior Warden
Edwin Emil Elser, P. M.................Treasurer
Homer Worthington Newman, P.M. Secretary
     Residence: 1146 M. H. del Pilar
       Phones: 2090 and 4429 P. O. Box 710
Walter Edward Coburn.....................Chaplain
Sidney Erickson.................................Marshal
Jackson William Archer..........Senior Deacon
Geoffrey Wainman Mayo........Junior Deacon
Solomon Libby.........................Senior Steward
Richard Oscar Williams..........Junior Steward
Francis James Brown..............................Tiler

STATED COMMUNICATIONS
Second Thursday each month

ANNUAL COMMUNICATION
December 12, 1918

Meets in Masonic Temple, The Escolta, Manila

BAGUMBAYAN LODGE No. 4, F. & A. M.—Manila

OFFICERS

Conrado Benitez................Worshipful **Master**
    Address: University of the Philippines
    Phones: 5414 and 4259.
Carlos Alejandro Barretto......Senior **Warden**
Francisco A. Delgado............Junior **Warden**
Vicente Trinos Acuña......................Treasurer
Leo Fischer..Secretary
    Residende: No. 1 Cortabitarte, Malate
    Phone: 830. P. O. Box: 1243
Exequiel Buenviaje Perez................Chaplain
Luiz Rafael Yangco............................Marshal ·
Fernando Gonzalez Sioco........Senior Deacon
Vicente Fabella...........................Junor Deacon
Herrman Carsen Luerssen......Senior Steward
José C. Velo.............................Junior Steward
Gregorio Eulogio José.........................Organist
B. John Mendez..................................Tiler

STATED COMMUNICATIONS
Second Wednesday each month

ANNUAL COMMUNICATION
December 11, 1918

Meets in Masonic Temple, The Escolta, Manila

ISLAND LODGE No. 5, F. & A. M.
FT. MILLS

OFFICERS

John Jerome Riehl...............................Master
    Residence: Fort Mills
    Business address c/o U. S. E. D.
    office Phone 266

Wilson Cairns Gardiner..........Senior Warden
Harry Mattox..........................Junior Warden
Mansel Elmore Heacock...................Treasurer
Clyde Baldwin Ely, P. M. ....Secretary
    Residence: Fort Mills
    Tel. 742

Ernest Adolph Reichardt..................Chaplain
Corbett Fitsimmons Reno......Senior Deacon
Walter Carl Schulze................Junior Deacon
Forrest Leonard Ritchey....................Marshal
Enrique Romero Martinez......Senior Steward
John Phillip Smith................Junior Steward
William Joura H. Lawrence...................Tiler

STATED COMMUNICATIONS
First Monday each month

ANNUAL COMMUNICATION
December 2, 1918

Meets in Spanish War Veterans Hall

SOUTHERN CROSS LODGE No 6,
F. & A. M.—Manila.

OFFICERS

Luther Boone Bewley......Worshipful Master
  (Absent)
John Frank Brown..............(Acting Master)
                          Senior Warden
  Office: Bureau of Audits
  Phone: 826
Omar Malcolm Shuman.............Junior Warden
Heinrich Wilhelm Gangnuss............Treasurer
Milton William Lazansky................Secretary
  Residence: 708 Vermont
  Phone: 4442
Bruce Simpson Wright......................Chaplain
William Andrew Weidmann......Senior Deacon
Eugene Arthur Perkins..........Junior Deacon
Clifford H. French..............................Marshal
Charles Francis Zeeck..........Senior Steward
Hubert Clark Lyman..............Junior Steward
Ernest I. Jeffery........................... ....Tiler

STATED MEETINGS
2nd Monday of each month

ANNUAL MEETING
First Monday in December

eets in Masonic Temple, The Escolta, Manila

BIAK-NA-BATO LODGE No. 7
F. & A. M.—Manila

OFFICERS

Felipe Tempongko.............Venerable Maestro
    Oficina La Estrella del Norte
     Phono 1047, P. O. Box 273
Joaquin Ventura...................Primer Vigilante
Dalmacio V. Monroy........Segundo Vigilante
A. V. de la Rosa................................Tesorero
Pastor M. de Guzman......................Secretario
    Oficina: Periodico ''El Ideal''
     Phone 1563, P. O. Box 600
Pedro Rodriguez...................................Capellan
José A. Ortega........................Primer Diacono
Francisco Gumila Carag......Segundo Diacono
B. A. Nolasco............Maestro de Ceremonias
Marcos Basa Concepcion........Primer Experto
Ponciano Buenaventura........Segundo Experto
Silvestre P. del Rosario....................Organista
Melecio de Leon....................Guarda Templo

STATED COMMUNICATIONS
2.o Viernes de cada mes

ANNUAL COMMUNICATION
13 de Diciembre, 1918

Meets in Masonic Temple, The Escolta, Manila
8

COSMOS LODGE No. 8, F. & A. M.
Manila

• OFFICERS

Walter A. Smith................Worshipful Master
    Residence: 1298 Agno
William D. Cheek.....................Senior Warden
Albert E. W. King....................Junior Warden
Filoteo Miranda................................ Treasurer
José Ma. Garcia...................................Secretary
    Phones: P. O. Box 415
Dexter L. Hazeltine.............................Chaplain
A. J. Hargis...............................Senior Deacon
Jeff C. Miller.............:.................Junior Deacon
Albert H. T. Carpenter......................Marshal
J. W. Ratliff.............................Senior Steward
Paul Dehn   ....Junior Steward
M. Herbert Burnham Jr. ....Tiler

STATED COMMUNICATIONS
First Wednesday each month

ANNUAL COMMUNICATION
December 4, 1918

Meets in Masonic Temple, The Escolta, Manila

9

ST. JOHN'S LODGE No. 9, F. & A. M. Manila

OFFICERS

William Frederick Gallin, Jr.......Worshipful
Master
Residence: No. 1483 Pennsylvania Ave
Phone 4488
Office Phone: 820
Joseph Russ...............................Senior Warden
Theodore Christian Zschokke Junior Warden
Daniel Denniston.............................Treasurer
Harris Frederick Mires....................Secretary
Residence: Manhattan Hotel, Phone 1072
Office, Phone No. 820.
Marvin Andrew Rader.........................Chaplain
Robert Frederick Barr.........................Marshal
William Russell Ramsey...........Senior Deacon
August Louis Prodoehl............Junior Deacon
Paul Martin Rasch................Senior Steward
Charles Henry Leavitt.............................Tiler

COMMUNICATIONS
1st and 3rd Fridays

ANNUAL COMMUNICATION
December 6, 1918

Meets in Masonic Temple, The Escolta, Manila
10

FAR EAST LODGE No. 10, F. & A. M.
Manila

OFFICERS

James McCombs Bury......Worshipful Master
    Residence: 234 Guerrero
    Phones: 4680 and 4800, P. O. Box 184
Harry Lawrence Noble............Senior Warden
William Henry Brown............Junior Warden
Edward Milham Ayers...................Treasurer
Warren Wallace Weston..................Secretary
    Residence: 548 San Luis
    Phone: 860, P. O. Box 1335
William H. Birt................................Chaplain
Elmer Drew Merrill................Senior Deacon
Samuel Barker...........................Junior Deacon
William H. Geagen............................Marshal
James R. Wright................................Steward
Ernest Woodall...................................Steward
Frank J. Scha i...Tiler

STATED COMMUNICATIONS
First Monday each month

ANNUAL COMMUNICATION
December 2, 1918

Meets in Masonic Temple, The Escolta, Manila

ILOILO LODGE No. 11, F. & A. M.
Iloilo

OFFICERS

Henry Francis Schuldt......Worshipful Master
Office: Visayan Drug Store.
Phone: 10, P. O. Box 217.

Eriberto Gonzalez y Nagar....Senior Warden

Charles B. Dodds......................Junior Warden

Engracio Padilla................................Treasurer

Francisco Javier Campos...................Secretary
Office: 86 Yznart
Phone; 236. P. O. Box 204

Marcelino Monfort Windham..Senior Deacon

Patricio Zaldarriaga.................Junior Deacon

Tomas Segovia y Olaybar......Senior Steward

Antonio Barrios Garcia.............................Tiler

STATED MEETINGS
Fourth Friday each month

STATED MEETINGS
December 27, 1918

Meets in Masonic Hall, Muelle Loney Iloilo, P.I.

NILAD LODGE No. 12, F & A. M.
Manila

OFFICERS

Teodoro M. Kalaw............Venerable Maestro
   Residence: 515 Peñafrancia, Paco
   Phones: 3923 and 830
Manuel Chaume.....................Primer Vigilante
Emiliano Quijano..............Segundo Vigilante
Bonifacio Mortell.................................Tesorero
Mariano Tenorio..............................Secretario
   Residence: 59 Sandejas, Pasay, Rizal
   Phones: 870 P. O. Box 828
Rafael Alunan .... Orador
Joaquin Garcia..........................Primer Experto
Aurelio L. Corcuera.............Segundo Experto
Crispin Montano............Limosnero u Hosp.∴
Ernest Ghulick.............1.er Maest.∴ Cerem.∴
Indalecio B. Crisostomo Guarda Templo
                             Intn.∴
Joaquin de San Agustin........Orador Adjunto
Francisco Geronimo.....2.o Maest.∴ Cerem.∴
Julian Ongcuangco......Maestro de Banquetes
Juan N. Aragon....Arq.∴ del Temp.∴ y Bib.∴
Chan Quep.................................Porta Estandarte
Ananias Taylo.......................................Heraldo
John M. Kossuth......Guarda Templo Externo
Mariano Gonzalez..................Primer Diacono
José S. Burgos.....................Segundo Diacono
Licerio Arcadio..........Arq.∴ Rev. de Cuentas

STATED MEETINGS
1st Saturday of each month

Meet at 843 Calle Lepanto, Sampaloc

WALANA LODGE No. 13, F. &. A. M.
Manila

OFFICERS

Felix Valencia....................Venerable Maestro
    Residence: 13 Quesaua, Tondo
(Vacant) ....Primer Vigilante
Santiago Santiago...............Segundo Vigilante
Julian Pajarillo.....................................Tesorero
Roman Lizardo.....................................Secretario
    Residence: 513 Benavides
    Phone: 5371
Elias Asuncion..Orador
Jeremias Relevante................Orador Adjunto
Manuel T. Alberto............Secretario Adjunto
Agapito Tuason.....................Tesorero Adjunto
Vicente Alivio..........................Primer Experto
Norberto Asinas....................Segundo Experto
Iluminado B. Planas...................Hospitalario
Godofredo del Rosario Maestro de
                                Ceremonias
Rafael de Jesus........Guarda Templo Interno
Claudio Carreon......Guarda Templo Externo
Isidro Alparaz.....................Arquitecto Revisor
Benito Ongtengco........Arquitecto del Templo
Alberto E. Soriaga................Primer Diacono
Higino T. Carranza...............Segundo Diacono
Victorino J. del Pilar...........Porta Estandarte
Leocadio Licop............Maestro de Banquetes

STATED COMMUNICATIONS
1st Wednesday of each month
Meet at Temple of Salomon, 1001 Bilbao.
Tondo.

14

SYMBOLIC

DALISAY LODGE No. 14, F. & A. M.
Manila

OFFICERS

Isidro R. Morales..............Venerable Maestro
    Residence: Plaza Miranda, Quiapo
    Phone: 968
José D. Mendoza............ .....Primer Vigilante
Ramon Peralta....................Segundo Vigilante
Cipriano Lara.......................................Tesorero
Domingo Ponce........... . ...Secretario
    Residence: 807 Sigay, Quiapo
Fortunato B. Rivera..............................Orador
Juan Anderson Hernandez......Primer Experto
Arsenio Reyes......................Segundo Experto
Esteban Munarriz......Maestro de Ceremonias
José P. Tagle......................................Limosnero
Roque Bautista..........Maestro de Banquetes
Doroteo L. Tercias....Guarda Templo Interno
Beato Castillo............Guarda Templo Externo
Vicente Mauricio................Porta Estandarte

STATED COMMUNICATIONS
First Thursday of every month

ANNUAL COMMUNICATION
Dec. 5, 1918

Meets at 838 Echague, Manila

15

-PILAR LODGE No. 15, F. & A. M.
Imus, Cavite

OFFICERS

Cand.do Sayoc.....................Venerable Maestro
      Residence: Imus, Cavite
      Phone: 137
Donato Virata.......................Primer Vigilante
Lorenzo B. Paredes...........Segundo Vigilante
Raymundo Reyes.....................................Tesorero
Pascual Magundayaw.........................Secretario
      Residence: Imus, Cavite
Julian F. Olaez.....................................Capellan
Patricio E. lel Rosario.........Primer Diacono
Mariano Dominguez.............Segundo Diacono
Felix Paredes.............Maestro de Ceremonias
Paulino Stuart.........................Primer Experto
Gonzalo Camantigue.............Segundo Experto
Angel Ramirez...........Guarda Templo Externo

STATED COMMUNICATIONS
Every 1st Saturday of each month

ANNUAL COMMUNICATION
December 1st, 1918

Meets at Imus, Cavite
16

SINUKUAN LODGE No. 16, F. & A. M. Manila

OFFICERS

Manuel L. Quezon..............Venerable Maestre
    Residence: 404 Lamayan, Santa Ana
Felipe Buencamino, Jr. ......Primer Vigilante
Mariano Yenko...................Segundo Vigilante
Pablo B. Herrera..................................Tesorero
Daniel Morelos......................................Secretario
    P. O. Box 809
Ricardo Gonzales Lloret......................Orador
Casalino A. Villas...................Primer Experto
José Santos...........................Segundo Experto
Julian Salgado........Limosnero u Hospitalario
Buenaventura Sasacas....Maestro de
                            Ceremonias
Vicente Liwanag........Maestro de Banquetes
Jacinto Herrera..........Arquitecto del Templo
Jacinto Damian........Guarda Templo Interno
Emilio Sancho..........Guarda Templo Externo

STATED COMMUNICATIONS ·

ANNUAL COMMUNICATION

Meets in Templo de Salomon, Calle Bilbao,
Tonlo
17

BAGONGBUHAY LODGE No. 17, F. & A. M.—Cavite

OFFICERS

Ladislao Diwa....................Venerable Maestro.
      Address: P. O. Box 26
Celestino Jacinto....................Primer Vigilante
José C. Sebastian.................Segundo Vigilante
Cirilo Regino...Tesorero
Emilio J. Basa...............................Secretario
      Address: P. O. Box 26
Fidel Tirona.............................Primer Experto
Simplicio Dionisio................Segundo Experto
August A. Reyes......................................Orador
Pablo A. Reyes..........Maestro de Ceremonias
Urbano Esteban............................Hospitalario
Honorato Cabug......................Guarda Templo
José N. Ramos.........................Primer Diacono
Joaquin Perez.........................Segundo Diacono

STATED COMMUNICATIONS

ANNUAL COMMUNICATION

Meets at San Roque, Cavite
18

ARAW LODGE No. 18, F. & A. M.
Manila

OFFICERS

Arsenio L. Gomez..............Venerable Maestro
    Residence: 905 Arlegui, Tondo
Ildefonso Villareal................Primer Vigilante
Angel M. Albert................Segundo Vigilante
Estanislao Feliciano.............................Tesorero
José M. Verdote................................Secretario
    Residence: 1010 A. Mabini, Malate
A. G. Barrion.......................................Orador
I. Hernandez......................Arquitecto Revisor
Francisco Sevilla....................Primer Diacono
F. Castañeda..........................Segundo Diacono
José Papa..............Limosnero u Hospitalario
Tirso Garcia..........................Primer Experto
Manuel I. Masanga.............Segundo Experto
Estanislao M. José....Maestro de Ceremonias
Bonifacio Ortega....................Archiv, Bibliot.
P. G. Ocampo............Guarda Templo Interno
Servillano Ocampo.................................Econ.

STATED COMMUNICATIONS
Second Tuesday of each month

ANNUAL COMMUNICATION
December, Second Tuesday

Meets at Temple of Salomon, 1001 Bilbao
Tondo
19

SILANGANAN LODGE No. 19, F. & A. M.—Pasig, Rizal

OFFICERS

Celestino Chaves................Venerable Maestro
    Residence: Pasig, Rizal
Ambrosio F. Zamora..........Primer Vigilante
Pedro Magsalin...................Segundo Vigilante
Elpidio L. Cruz....................................Tesorero
Juan R. Avelino...............................Secretario
    Residence: Sagad, Pasig, Rizal
    Office: Executive Bureau, Manila
    Telephone: 830
Felino Guevara.........................Primer Diacono
Mateo D. Cipriano................Segundo Diacono
Leandro A. Jabson....Primer Maestro de
                              Ceremonias
Vicente Morada.........................Primer Experto
Marcelino M. Cruz................Segundo Experto
Honorio Musni...Orador
Pablo Umali.................Limosnero Hospitalario
Simplicio, Manalo...................Porta Estandarte
Mateo Guerrero...................Arquitecto Revisor
Fernando Caruncho..................Orador Adjunto
Pedro C. Jabson................Secretario Adjunto
Gregorio Flores....Segundo Maest. de Cerem.
Vicente J. Victorio......Maestro de Banquetes
Francisco Kintos........Guarda Templo Interno
Emiliano Caruncho....Guarda Templo Externo

STATED COMMUNICATIONS
First Saturday of each month
ANNUAL COMMUNICATION
December 7, 1918
20

RIZAL LOPEZ LODGE No. 20, F. & A. M.—Lopez, Tayabas

OFFICERS

Alfonzo Riobo.....................Venerable **Maestro**
P. O. Box 20
Victor Oblefias.....................Primer Vigilante
Hipolito E. Valeña...............Segundo Vigilante
Joaquin de Arano..................................Tesorero
Uldarico Villamor............................Secretario
P. O. Box 20
Getulio Capistrano...................................Orador
Maximo Morales.......................Primer Experto
Esteban David.......................Seguno Experto
Bonifacio Tabien........Maestro de Ceremonias
Rafael Marquez......Limosnero u Hospitalario
Inocencio Caparros.:..........Arquitecto Revisor
Mariano L. Barrameda....Maest. de Banquetes
Espiridion Arguelles..............Porta Estandarte
Emilio Season..Heraldo
Rosendo L. Nicuesa....Guarda Templo Interno
Delfin Villasanta......Guarda Templo Externo
Aracadio Veracruz..................Orador Adjunto
Eustacio A. Escobar........Secretario Adjunto
Pedro V. Florido....Maest. de Cerem. Adjunto

STATED COMMUNICATIONS

ANNUAL COMMUNICATION

DAPITAN LODGE No. 21, F. & A. M.
Manila

OFFICERS

Mariano Santos...................Venerable Maestro
   Resdience: 1017 Misericordia
Esteban de Guzman............Primer Vigilante
Vicente Tagudin.................Segundo Vigilante
Hilario Cameña......................................Tesorero
Sixto Ongchangco..............................Secretario
   Residence: 512 Economia, Sampaloc
Pablo Pargas...............................Primer Experto
Hermogenes Ilagan.................Segundo Experto
Pedro Aza Cruz.........................Primer Diacono
Carlos Maglaya........................Segundo Diacono
Andres Castillejos......Maestro de Ceremonias
Remigio G. Garcia....Guarda Templo Interno
Marcos Garcia..........Guarda Templo Externo
Marcelino Vera...Orador
Carlos Borja.......................................Limosnero

STATED COMMUNICATIONS
First Monday of each month

ANNUAL COMMUNICATION
December 2, 1918

Meets at Temple of Salomon, 1001 Bilbao,
Tondo·
22

RIZAL MANILA LODGE No. 22, F. & A. M.—Manila

OFFICERS

Francisco Zamora................Venerable Maestro
   Residence: 804 Soler
   Phones: 4005 and 980

Luciano Dantis......................Primer Vigilante

Marciano Guevara..............Segundo Vigilante

Miguel Unson..Tesorero

José V. Mariño....................................Secretario
   Residence: 168 Magallanes. W. C.
   Phones: 5323 and 980 P. O. Box 153

Feliciano Basa.......................................Orador

Mariano Pacheco...................................Experto

Domiciano Sandoval....Maestro de Ceremonias

Florentino Serra....Guarda Templo Interno y
       Maestro de Banquetes

Roman Sarmiento.......................................Tiler

STATED COMMUNICATIONS
Tercer Miercoles de cada mes

ANNUAL COMMUNICATION
18 de Diciembre, 1918

23

SOLIDARIDAD LODGE, No. 23, F. & A. M.

OFFICERS

Prudencio A. Remigio,......Venerable Maestro.
    Residencia: 1249 Oroquieta, Sta. Cruz.
    Oficina: 211 Carriedo, Sta. Cruz
    Telefono: 3255
José S. Galvez, ...Primer Vigilante
Filemon Cosio, ...Segundo Vigilante
Modesto Joaquin, ...Orador
Andrés Trujillo, ...Secretario
    Residencia: 314 Sulucan, Sampaloc
    Telefono 3340
Matias Santos, ...Tesorero
Benito Dominguez, ·   .Primer Experto
Juan M. Ramos, ...Limosnero Hos pltalario
Lorenzo Javier,   ...   Primer Maestro
                      de Ceremonias
José F. Ramos, ...Orador Adjunto
Julian Castro, ...Secretario Adjunto
      Segundo Maestro de Ceremonias
Emilio Pestaño, ...   Arquitecto Revisador
Luis Pery,   ..Guarda Templo Interno
Francisco Tolentini, ..Guarda Templo Externo

STATED COMMUNICATIONS

Tenida ordinaria: Tercer Sábado de cada mes

ANNUAL COMMUNICATION
Primer Sábado de Diciembre

Meets in 843 Lepanto, Sampaloc

BANAHAW LODGE No. 24, F. & A. M.
Atimonan, Tayabas

Osmundo Alberto..............Venerable Maestro
    Residence: No. 4 Calle Independencia,
    Atimonan, Tayabas
Teofilo Gregorio......................Primer Vigilante
Luis R. Manalo.:.............:....Segundo Vigilante
Alejandro F. Pilar..............................Tesorero
Victor Amador...Secretario
    P. O. Box 1, Atimonan, Tayabas
Eleuterio Campomanes........................Capellan
Gregorio Orda..Orador
Roman Montenegro...................Primer Diacono
Luis N. Racelis....................Segundo Diacono
Isidro Campomanes....Maestro de Ceremonias
Diosdado Amado,....................Primero Experto
Urbano Lota............................Segundo Experto
Esteban Montenegro Guarda Templo Externo

STATED COMMUNICATIONS
First Saturday of each month

ANNUAL COMMUNICATION
December 7, 1918

Meets at Templo Masonico, Calle Taft 6,
Atimonan

MALINAW LODGE No. 25, F. & A. M.
San Pablo, Laguna

OFFICERS

Marcial Alimario..Master
P. O. Box 7
Marciano Brion............................Senior Warden
Gregorio Laurel........................Junior Warden
Damian Magpantay............................Treasurer
Pablo G. Ticzon................................Secretary
P. O. Box 7
Miguel Leonor..Chaplain
Felix Hocson............................Senior Deacon
Hermenegildo Devesa..............Junior Deacon
Antonio Aguirre..Marshal
Meliton Brion..Steward
Mariano V. Santos....................................Orator
Inocencio Barleta..Tiler

STATED COMMUNICATIONS

ANNUAL COMMUNICATION

PINAGSABITAN LODGE No. 26, F. & A. M.—Santa Cruz, Laguna

OFFICERS

José M. Quintero................Venerable Maestro
P. O. Box 17, Sta. Cruz, Laguna
Vicente Rivera Sayo............Primer Vigilante
Francisco Alfonso............ ....segundo Vigilante
Vicente C. Reventar......... ....:......Tesorero
Santos Carmelo..................................Secretario
P. O. Box 17, Sta. Cruz. Lalaguna
Amado Saul..Capellan
Pedro Resurreccion...............Primer Diacono
Nicasio José............................Segundo Diacono
Gaudencio Tesoro....................Primer Experto
Anastasio Olivares................Segundo Experto
Sebastian Pamatmat..Maestro de Ceremonias
Juan Calcotas............Guarda Templo Externo
José A. Dimayuga..................................Orador
José Zaguirre..Auditor

STATED COMMUNICATIONS
First Saturday of each month

ANNUAL COMMUNICATION
December 15, 1918

Meets at Calle F. Sario, Santa Cruz, Laguna

BAGUMBAYAN MANILA LODGE
No. 27, F. & A, M,—Manila

OFFICERS

José Elchico..........................Venerable Maestro
          Residence: 513 Lavesarez
          Phone: 8039
Francisco A. de Asis............Primer Vigilante
Patricio M. Cruz.................Segundo Vigilante
Francisco de Leon.................................Tesorero
Gonzalo Torrente.................................Secretario
          Residence: 1014 Lavezares
          Phone: 8599
Pablo Reyes y Castillo..........Primer Experto
Pascual de Leon...................Segundo Experto
Tomas Lorenzo.................................Orador
Francisco Hernandez..Maestro de Ceremonias
Ramon A. Maneja..........................Hospitalario
Moises San Juan.................Porta Estandarte
Maximo R. Santiago..............Guarda Templo

STATED COMMUNICATIONS
First Saturday of each month

ANNUAL COMMUNICATION

Templo de Salomon, Calle Bilbao, Tondo

BALINTAWAK LODGE No. 28,
F. & A. M.—Gumaca, Tayabas

OFFICERS

Antonio E. Argosino..........Venerable Maestro
Residence: Quezon, Tayabas
Gerardo L. Tañada................Primer Vigilante
Felix S. Adad....................Segundo Vigilante
Victoriano A. Tañafranca..................Tesorero
Panfilo Tañada.....................................Secretario
Residence: Gumaca, Tayabas
Aurelio Nava...Capellan
Anastasio Martinez..................Primer Diacono
Francisco Ramso..................Segundo Diacono
Marciano Principe......Maestro de Ceremonias
Mariano Barretto....................Primer Experto
Deogracias A. Tañada..........Segundo Experto

STATED COMMUNICATIONS
The 2nd Saturday of every month.

ANNUAL COMMUNICATION
The 2nd Saturday of December

Lodge meets at the Masonic Temple, Gumaca,
Tayabas, P. I.
29

ZAPOTE LODGE No. 29, F. & A. M.
Rosario, Cavite

OFFICERS

Santiago M. Salazar..........Venerabie Maestro
Residence: Rosario, Cavite
Sabas P. Alcid.....................Primer Vigilante
Tomas Rodriguez................Segundo Vigilante
Eugenio A. Yuvieneo...........................Tesorero
Graciano P. Pugay.............................Secretario
Residence: Rosario, Cavite
Luis Titonjua....................................Instructor
Claro S. Basa...........................Primer Experto
Pedro B. Punzalan................Segundo Experto
Amado Prudente........Maestro de Ceremonias
Gavino Topacio...............................Hospitalario
Eulalio Raymundo........Maestro de Banquetes
Emilio Guevarra........Guarda Templo Externo

STATED COMMUNICATIONS
First Saturday of each month

ANNUAL COMMUNICATION
December 7, 1918

MAKTAN LODGE No 30, F. & A. M.
Cebu, Cebu

OFFICERS

Alfonso Raquel......................Venerable Maestro
P. O. Box 31

Henry U. Umstad..................Primer Vigilante
Miguel Simon.......................Segundo Vigilante
Anastasio S. Rama.............................Tesorero
Mariano G. del Rosario...................Secretario
P. O. Box 31

José N. Solón.....................Secretario Interino
José N. Solón..............Maestro de Ceremonias
Pantaleon E. del Rosario....Maestro de Ceremonias Interino
Saturnino D. Villoria..............Primer Diacono
Joaquin Alix...........................Segundo Diacono
Eugenio S. del Rosario........................Orador
Martin Lorenzo........................Primer Experto
Marcial Borromeo...................Segundo Experto
Policarpio Cepeda..........Primer Maest. Banq.
Jose N. Solon..Segundo Maest. de Banquete
Joaquin Alix..............Guarda Templo Interno
Victorino Reynes......Guarda Templo Externo

STATED COMMUNICATIONS
Every first Friday of the month.

ANNUAL COMMUNICATION

Meets at Lodge Hall, Corner of Calles Magallanes and Plaridel.

MAGDALO LODGE No. 31, F. & A. M.
Kawit, Cavite

OFFICERS

Felix Cajulis.........................Venerable Maestro
    Office: Bureau of Internal Revenue
Julian Balmaseda...................Primer Vigilante
Canuto Encarnacion.............Segundo Vigilante
Anastasio Legaspi...................................Tesorero
Daniel Sambong................................Secretario
    Residence: Binakayan, Cavite
Emiliano T. Tirona................................Orador
Emilio P. Virata.....................Orador Adjunto
Leon Manalo.................Maestro de Ceremonias
Silvestre Vales......maest. de Cerem. Adjunto
Francisco Gaudier....................................Experto
Vicente Lagda.........................Experto Adjunto
Pedro Bagalawis........Guarda Templo Interno
Felipe Peregrino........Guarda Templo Externo
Servillano H. Palugod........................Capellan
Felix Savas...Limosnero
Maximo Diaz.......................Limosnero Adjunto

STATED COMMUNICATIONS

ANNUAL COMMUNICATION

MARTIRES DEL 96 LODGE No. 32, F. & A. M.—Nagcarlan, Laguna

OFFICERS

Jose Lucido............................Venerable Maestro
    Residence: Nagcarlan
Ramon Cabezas....................Primer Vigilante
Aproniano de la Peña........Segundo Vigilante
Casiano Placente.................................Tesorero
Sinforoso Sollorano...........................Secretario
    Residence: Nagcarlan
Juan Arcegal.......................................Capellan
Juan Bujalance.........................Primer Diacono
Fermin D. Buan....................Segundo Diacono
Carlos Vita.................Maestro de Ceremonias
Crisanto M. Gusayko.............................Orador
Feliz Chipongian......................Prmer Experto
Jose Plantilla.........................Segundo Experto
Pedro Monserrat........Limosnero Hospitalario
Felix Poon.............................Porta Estandarte
Agustin Vista............Guarda Templo Interno
Ramiro Esmilla..........Guarda Templo Externo
Jose Plantilla..Organista
Mariano Monserrat......Archivero-Bibliotecario
Candido Carriaga.............................Arquitecto
Angel Tuico..................Maestro de Banquetes

STATED COMMUNICATIONS
First Saturday of each Month

ANNUAL COMMUNICATION

Meets at its Temple on Gral. Luna St.,
Nagcarlan

ISAROG LODGE No. 33. F. & A. M.
Naga, Ambos Camarines

OFFICERS

Julian Ocampo....................Venerable Maestro
    Residence: Naga, Ambos Camarines
Mariano L. de la Rosa......Primer Vigilante
Fernando Alvarez.................Segundo Vigilante
Emeterio Abella.....................................Tesorero
Juan San Buenaventura....................Secretario
    Residence: Naga, Ambas Camarines
José Borja...Capellan
William Neill..............Maestro de Ceremonias
Santiago Rodrigo....................Primer Diacono
Ramon Enrile........................Segundo Diacono
Judge H. Oswald......................Primer Experto
Hermenegildo Miraflor..........Segundo Experto
Eugenio I. Ocampo.............................Organista
Mariano Dy Liacco.................Guarda Templo

STATED COMMUNICATIONS
Segundo Viernes de cada mes 5 p. m.

ANNUAL COMMUNICATION
Segundo viernes del mes de Diciembre

Meets on Calle General Luna

LINCOLN LODGE No. 34, F. & A. M.
Olongapo, Zambales

OFFICERS

Leandro G. Salvador........Venerable Maestro
P. O. Box 4C
Francisco Castro....................Primer Vigilante
Jose San Lorenzo................Segundo Vigilante
Eusebio H. Lorenzana........................Tesorero
Catalino Santos.................................Secretario
Office, Supply Department, Olongapo

STATED COMMUNICATIONS

ANNUAL COMMUNICATION

BATANGAS LODGE No. 35, F. & A. M.—Batangas, Batangas

OFFICERS

Juan M. Gutierrez............Venerable Maestro
        P. O. Box Batangas
Juan Muños..........................Primer Vigilante
Sisenando Ferriols............Segundo Vigilante
Juan Palacios...Tesorero
Juan Carag...Secretario
        Residences: Box 5, Batangas
Celestino Aragon....................................Capellan
Liberato Evangelista..............Primer Diacono
Francisco Villarosa..............Segundo Diacono
Federico Romero....Maestro de Ceremonias y
                Archivero Bibliotecario
Mariano Dagli.......................Primer Experto
Apolonio Abad.......................Segundo Experto
Simeon Babasa........Guarda Templo Externo
José Villanueva.....................................Orador
Mariano Vega.......................................Organista
Zacarias Canent........Maestro de Banquetes
Venancio Trinidad............Arquitecto Revisor
Pastor R. Mayo....................Porta. Estandarte
Aquino Deras............Guarda Templo Interno

STATED COMMUNICATIONS
Tercer Sabado de cada mes

ANNUAL COMMUNICATION
Diciembre 21, 1918.

Meets at Templo Masonico, Calle P. Pelaez,
Batangas

REGENERACION LODGE No. 36, F. & A. M.—Tar'ac, Tarlac

OFFICERS

Manuel de Leon..................Venerable Maestro
      Residence: Tarlac, Tarlac
Salvador G. Estrada............Primer Vigilante
Francisco Urrutia..............Segundo Vigilante
Jose Ramos...Tesorero
Jose S. Bañuelos..............................Secretario
      P. O. Box 15
Arturo Dancel..Orador
Francisco Villanueva..............Primer Experto
Gonzalo P. Aquino................Segundo Experto
Anastacio Cura.................................Limosnere
Deogracias Tañedo....Maestro de Ceremonias
Ramon Tañedo.....................Arquitecto Revisor
Vicente Tabamo............Maestro de Banquete
Ignacio Cura..............Arquitecto del Templo
Francisco Cruz.......................Porta Estandarte
Quirino Antonio...................................Heraldo
Lino Ignacio..............Guarda Templo Interior
Rafael Ceballos.....................Primer Diacono
Manuel Salak........................Segundo Diacono
Prudencio Tañedo..............Secretario Adjunto
Cornelio Pascual..................Tesorero Adjunto
Sisenando Palarca..................Orador Adjunto

STATED COMMUNICATIONS

1st Saturday of each month

ANNUAL COMMUNICATION

Saturday preceeding the Feast of St. John
the Evangelis

Meets in Masonic Temple Tarlac

KALILAYAN LODGE No. 37,
F. & A. M.—Lucena, Tayabas

OFFICERS

Federico M. Unson...........Venerable Maestro
      Residence: Lucena. Tayabas
Eusebio G. Dimaano............Primer Vigilante
Ambrosio Panganiban........Segundo Vigilante
A. M. Ginainati................................Tesorero
Filemon N. Caperiña........................Secretario
      Residence: Lucena, Tayabas
Pedro M. Nieva......................................Orador
Honorio Lanuza....................................Capellan
Graciano Font ....Primer Diacono
José Estagle...........................Segundo Diacono
Ariston S. Zamora......Maestro de Ceremonias
Eligio Magallanes...................Primer Experto
Benito Querol........................Segundo Experto
Pedro Pulgado........Guarda Templo Experno
Toribio Lacza....................................Limosnero
Francisco de Jesus..............Porta Estandarte

STATED COMMUNICATIONS
Last Saturday of each month

ANNUAL COMMUNICATION
November 30th, 1918

Meets at its Temple in Lucena

BULUSAN LODGE No. 38, F. & A. M.
Sorsogon, Sorsogon

OFFICERS

Bernabe Flores.................Venerable Maestro
     Residence: Sorsogon

Leoncio Grajo........................Primer Vigilante

Jose Figueroa...................:.Segundo Vigilante

Mariano Olondriz...................................Tesorero

Jose E. de Vera.............................Secretario
     P. O. Box 13, Sorsogon.

STATED COMMUNICATIONS

ANNUAL COMMUNICATION

MABINI LODGE No. 39, F. & A. M.
Aparri, Cagayan

OFFICERS

Fermin Macanaya..............Venerable Maestro
       P. O. Box 27, Aparri, Cagayan
Nemesio Furagganan............Primer Vigilante
José Gonzales.....................Segundo Vigilante
Marcelino Kalaya................................Tesorero
José C. Foz..Secretario
       P. O. Box 27, Aparri, Cagayan
José de los Reyes...............................Capellan
Isabelo Yabut......................... Primer Diacono
Raymundo Concepcion..........Segundo Diacono
Amando E. Foz..........Maestro de Ceremonias
Fares Chebat...........................Maestro Adjunto
Pedro Aguila............................Primer Experto
Salvador Torra.....................Segundo Experto
Hermogenes Florentino....Guarda Templo Ex.
Francisco Umengan....Guarda Templo Interno
Gregorio Littaua.............Orador, Bibliotecario
Ramon Villasanta.....................Orador Adjunto
José Santos...Heraldo
Tirso Macabangun......Limosnero Hospitalario
Fernando P. Lopez.............Arquitecto Revisor
Ignacio Reyes...............Maestro de Banquetes
Alejandro Alvarado.............................Organista

STATED COMMUNICATIONS

ANNUAL COMMUNICATION

MAGINDANAW LODGE No. 40, F. & A. M.—Cagayan de Misamis

OFFICERS

Apolinar ,Velez Ramos......Venerable Maestro
Residence: Cagayan de Misamis
Nemesio Chaves....................Primer Vigilante
Tomas Felix Nery..............Segundo Vigilante
Juan Roa Valdeconcha..Inspector de Distrito
Zacarias Tottoc...................................Tesorero
Jose Gallofin.......................................Secretario
Residence: Cagayan de Misamis
Emilio Pineda................Capellan y Orador
Antonio Baz..............................Primer Diacono
Rito Islao...............................Segundo Diacono
Clemente Chaves........Maestro de Ceremonias
Celedonio T. Abellanosa........Primer Experto
Gregorio G. Bella...................Segundo Experto
Nicanor M. Velez......Guarda Templo Externo

STATED COMMUNICATIONS
First Saturday of each month

ANNUAL COMMUNICATION
December 7, 1918

Meets at Masonic Temple, Calle Real, es-
quina a la Calle Visayas, Cagayan, Misamis

MINERVA LODGE No. 41, F & A. M.
Manila

OFFICERS

Salvador Chofre................Venerable Maestro
     El Hogar Filipino   ᐟ
Adolfo Aenlle........................Primer Vigilante
Gabriel Tabalon...................Segundo Vigilante
Heinrich A. C. Mueller....................Tesorero
Matias Garcia......................................Secretario
Manuel Escudero....................................Orador
Jose Garau...............................Primer Experto
Jacinto Ocampo....................Segundo Experto
Felix Calvo........Primer Maes. de Ceremonias
Celso Llobregat........Segundo Maes. de Cere.
Enrique Lopez Mena....Maestro de Banquetes
Emmanuel Strauss....Limosnero Hospitalario
Ildefonso Santos Reyes....Secretario Adjunto
Jacob J. Handelsman..Guarda Templo Interno
Joaquin Carrion......Guarda Templo Externo
               y Arquitecto Revisor

STATED COMMUNICATIONS

ANNUAL COMMUNICATION

Meets in Temp'o de Salomon, 1001 Bilbao,
Tondo, Manila

NOLI ME TANGERE LODGE No. 42,
F. & A. M.—Pasay, Rizal.

OFFICERS

Manuel de Santos............Venerable Maestro
 Residence 1019 Aceyteros, Tondo
 Phone 8203
Adam D. Tanner..................Primer Vigilante
Isabelo Concepcion............Segundo Vigilante
Pedro M. Poblete..............................Tesorero
José P. Parraga...............................Secretario
 Residence: 88 M. H. del Pilar
 Pasay, Rizal. Phone: 4559
Dionisio San Agustin..............Primer Experto
Julian Bella...........................Segundo Experto
Faustino Inocencio....Maestro de Ceremonias
Macario de Castro......................Hospitalario
Gabino Fernando....................Primer Diacono
Paterno Lopez......................Segundo Diacono
Severo A. Esculto........Arquitecto del Templo
Braulio Adao............Guarda Templo Interno
Elias Gamban............Guarda Templo Externo
Damaso Reyes..............Maestro de Banquetes
Maximo A. Madridejos............Orador Adjunto
Alejandro Hernandez..........Porta Estandarte

STATED COMMUNICATIONS
First Saturday of each month

ANNUAL COMMUNICATION
December 7, 1918

Meets at Pasay, Rizal

TAYABAS LODGE No. 43,
Tayabas, Tayabas

OFFICERS

Teodoro Dolendo...................................Master
        Residence: Tayabas, Tayabas

Vicente Ragudo.........................Senior Warden

Luis Mallari.............................Junior Warden

Sergio E. Caparros.............................Secretary
        Residence: Tayabas, Tayabas

STATED COMMUNICATIONS
. .

ANNUAL COMMUNICATION

Meets at Masonic Hall, Tayabas

CHARLESTON LODGE, U. D.,
Agana, Guam

OFFICERS

H. S. Merchant..................................Secretary

This Lodge has been recently formed and no information has been obtained regarding its officers.

MOUNT APO LODGE, U. D., F. & A. M.—Zamboanga

OFFICERS

James Wilson...Master
    Residence: San Jose Road, Zamboanga
    Phone: 33
R. T. McCutchen......................Senior Warden
E. M. Saleeby..........................Junior Warden
F. P. Williamson..............................Treasurer
A. W. Crosby.....................................Secretary
    Residence: Calle Magallanes, Zamboanga
    Phone: 14
James Logan..............................Senior Deacon
Eduardo Montenegro.................Junior Deacon
C. M. Spears...................................Marshal
Andres Pastor..........................Senior Steward
Manuel Blanco........................Junior Steward
W. F. Scheben..Tiler

STATED COMMUNICATIONS
First Thursday of each month

ANNUAL COMMUNICATION

46

MALOLOS LODGE U. D.,
Malolos, Bulacan

OFFICERS

Nicolas Buendia................Venerable Maestro

Sotero Bayot...........................Primer Vigilante

Juan Dominguez...............Segundo Vigilante

Amado V. Aldaba...............................Secretari٠
  Address: Provincial Treasury Building

This lodge has been organized since the meeting of the Grand Lodge.

LODGE PERLA DEL ORIENTE
No. 1034, S. C. A. F. & A. M.
Manila, P. I.

OFFICERS BEARERS FOR 1918

Frank H. Hale.................Worshipful Master
    Residence: 302 Amadeo, Paco
    Office: Exchange Shoe Co. Phone: 1924
Bruce L. Crossby..................Senior Warden
Ed. P. Wyruchowski.............Junior Warden
Charles A. Tansill..........................Secretary
    Office: Bureau of Public Works
    Phone: 870
P. G. Blanc...........................Treasurer
Newton Cofer...........................Chaplain
Henry Brown.................Senior Deacon
L. de Pablas...................Junior Deacon
O. Squalcintini.............Master of Ceremonies
P. C. Miller...............................Organist
I. S. Reyes.....................Inner Guard
John Arville..................................Tyler
Victor Johnson.........................Steward
Ed. J. Hawkes........................Steward

STATED MEETINGS
First Saturday of each month

ANNUAL MEETING

Meets at Pickett Hall, Plaza Santa Cruz,
Manila
48

CAPITULAR

LUZON CHAPTER No. 1, R. A. M.
Manila

Subordinate to the General Grand Chapter
R. A. M. of the U. S. A.

OFFICERS

Edward E. Elser...........................High Priest
     Residence: 437 Looban
     Phones: 129 and 637
Charles A. Tansill.............................King
Stanton Youngberg........................Scribe
Enrique A. Aced..........................Treasurer
Newton C. Comfort, P. H. P. ....Secretary
     Residence: 128 San Luis
     Phones: 28 and 4306
Frank P. Thornton........Captain of the Host
Sidney Erickson...............Principal Sojourner
F. A. Stevenson..............Royal Arch Captain
Lovett M. Nichols........Master of the 3d Vail
William H. Brown......Master of the 2d Vail
Chas. H. W. Aitken....Master of the 1st Vail
David Fletcher.........................Sentinel

STATED CONVOCATIONS
Third Monday each month

ANNUAL CONVOCATION
December 16. 1918

Meet in Masonic Temple, The Escolta, Manila
49

ORIENTAL COUNCIL No. 1, R.& S. M·
Manila

Subordinate to the Grand Council
R. & S. M. of the U. S. A.

OFFICERS

Newton C. Comfort............Illustrious Master
        Residence: 128 San Luis
        Phones: 28 and 4306
Edwin E. Elser........................Deputy Master
Eugene M. Barton..Prinl. Condr. of the Work
Aziz T. Hashim................................Treasurer
Joshua T. Colvin................................Secretary
        Office: City Hall
William H. Chapman....Captain of the Guard
Charles A. Tansill........Conductor of Council
Lovett M. Nichols..............................Steward
Warren W. Weston...........................Chaplain
Ernest W. MacReady...........................Sentinel

STATED ASSEMBLIES
Fourth Friday each month

ANNUAL ASSEMBLY
December 27, 1918

Meets in Masonic Temple, The Escolta, Manila
50

FAR EAST COMMANDERY No. 1
KNIGHTS TEMPLAR—Manila

Subordinate to the Grand Encampment
Knights Templar of the U. S. A.

OFFICERS

Em.Sir and Rev.Bruce S.Wright. Commander
　　　Residence: 222 Arquiza
　　　Phone: 3546
Sir James F. Kemp..... .. ..Generalismo
Sir William F. Gallin, Jr.....Captain General
Sir Stanton Youngberg..........Senior Warden
Sir Christian W. Rosenstock..Junior Warden
Eminent Sir Milton
　　　E. Springer.....................Prelate Emeritus
Sir Harry J. Morgan..............................Prelate
Sir Frederic H. Stevens......Associate Prelate
Eminent Sir Edwin E. Elser.............Treasurer
　　　Residence: 128 San Luis
　　　Phones: 28 and 4306
Sir Enrique A. Aced..............Standard Bearer
Sir Frederick A. Stevenson....Sword Bearer
Sir Ernest MacReady.............................Warder
Sir William H. Chapman............Third Guard
Sir Francis Kane.........................Second Guard
Sir Sidney Erickson.....................First Guard
Sir John C. Howe................................Organist
Sir Joshua T. Colvin...........................Sentinel

STATED CONCLAVES
First Saturday each month

ANNUAL CONCLAVES
December 7, 1918

Meets in Masonic Temple, The Escolta, Manila

MT. ARAYAT LODGE OF PERFEC-TION No. 1, (4° to 14°)—Manila

Owes allegiance to the Supreme Council A. & A. S. R., Southern Jurisdiction, U. S. A.

OFFICERS

Newton C. Comfort, 32°....Venerable Master
        Residence: 128 San Luis
        Phones: 28 and 4306
George R.Harvey, 32°K.C.C.H.SeniorWarden
Charles S. Banks, 32°............Junior Warden
Chester G. Gerkin, 32°.......................Orator
Edwin E. Elser, 32°...........................Almoner
Warren W. Weston, 32°K.C.C.H.....Secretary
Aziz T. Hashim, 32°.......................Treasurer
Walter J. Grodske, 32° Master of Ceremonies
Frank P. Thornton, 32°.....................Expert
Charles M. Colton 32°........Assistant Expert
William A. Weidmann,32°Capt.of the Guard
Frank W. Towle 32°..............................Tiler

REGULAR MEETINGS
Second Friday each month

ANNUAL MEETING
February 14, 1919

Meets in Masonic Temple, The Escolta, Manila

LAKANDOLA LODGE OF PERFEC. TION No. 2,—Manila

Owes allegiance to the Supreme Council A. & A. S. R., Southern Jurisdiction, U. S .A.

OFFICERS

Tomas Earnshaw, 32º........Venerable Master
   Residence: Passay Beach, Pasay, Rizal.
   Phone: 3156
Albino Sy Cip 32º...............Senior Warden
Leoncio L. Espino, 32º........Junior Warden
Teodoro M. Kalaw, 32º.........................Orator
Enrique P. Brías Roxas, 32º............Almoner
Daniel Morelos, 32º.........................Secretary
   P. O. Box 809.
Jose Fabella 18º.............................Treasurer
Pablo B. Herrera, 32º..Master of Ceremonies
Manuel Xeres-Burgos, Jr. 30º............Expert
Mariano Tenorio, 30º..........Assistant Expert
José Topacio, 30º........Captain of the Guard
Bonifacio Mortell, 30º..............................Tiler
John C. Howe 32º...........................Organist

REGULAR MEETINGS
Fourth Friday of each month

ANNUAL MEETINGS

Meets in Masonic Temple, The Escolta, Manila

MANU CHAPTER OF ROSE CROIX
No. 1, (15° to 18°)—Manila

Owes allegiance to the Supreme Counci
A. & A. S. R., Southern Jurisdiction, U. S .A

OFFICERS

Chester J. Gerkin, 32°............Wise Maste
      Residence: 923 Indiana
      Phones: 2124 and 2125
Geoffrey W. Mayo 32°............Senior Warde
Charles S. Banks, 32°............Junior Warde
Charles A. Tansil 32°, K.C.C.H.:.........Orato
Edwin E. Elser, 32°..........................Almoue
Warren W. Weston 32°.,K.C.C.H...Secretar
      Residence: 548 San Luis
Aziz T. Hashim, 32°..... ,..............Treasure
Walter J. Grodske, 32°Master of Ceremonie
Eugene A. Perkins, 32°.........................Exper
Robert E. Hall, 32°............Assistant Exper
Fred M. Harden, 32............Standard Beare
Fred C. Lawrence, 32°Guardian of the Templ
Frank W. Towle, 32°................................Tile

REGULAR MEETINGS

ANNUAL MEETING

Meets in Masonic Temple, The Escolta, Manil

BURGOS CHAPTER OF ROSE CROIX, No. 2,—Manila

Owes allegiance to the Supreme Council A. & A. S. R., Southern Jurisdiction, U. S .A.

OFFICERS

H. Lawrence, Noble 32°............Wise Master
      Residence: 1016 Taft Avenue
      Phone: 4888
Conrado Benitez 30°...............Junior Warden
Alfonso Sy Cip. 32°................Senior Warden
Emilio Aguinaldo, 32°............................Orator
Enrique P. Brias Roxas, 32°...........Almoner
Leo Fischer 32° K.C.C.H. ....Secretary
      Residence: 1 Cortabitarte, Malate
      Phone: 3480. P. O. Box 1284
Omar M. Shuman, 32°...................Treasurer
Artemas L. Day, 32°....Master of Ceremonies
Manuel Camus, 32°, K.C.C.H...............Expert
Ernest Guhlick, 30°............Assistant Expert
Walter Bruggmann, 30°........Standard Bearer
Filoteo R. Miranda, 32°....Guardian of the
                                    Temple
Samuel Barker, 30°.................................Tiler
John C. Howe, 32°...........................Organist

REGULAR MEETINGS
Fourth Friday of each month

ANNUAL MEETING

Meets in Masonic Temple. The Escolta. Manila

SCOTTISH RITE

CONFUCIUS COUNCIL OF KADOSH, No. 1, (19° to 30°)—Manila

Owes allegiance to the Supreme Council
A. & A. S. R., Southern Jurisdiction, U. S .A.

OFFICERS

Edwin E. Elser,, 32°..........................Preceptor
      Residence: 437 Looban
      Phones: 637 and 8129
Walter J. Grodske, 32°....1st Sub. Preceptor
Geoffrey W. Mayo, 32°....2nd Sub. Preceptor
Charles A. Tansill, 32° K.C.C.H. Chancellor
Wade C. West, 32°.................................Orator
Enrique Aced. 32°..............................Almoner
      Residence: 548 San Luis
Warren W. Weston, 32°K.C.C.H. Registrar
Aziz T. Hashim, 32°.....................:..Treasurer
Luther B. Bewley, 32° Master of Ceremonies
Frank M. Harden, 32°..........................Draper
C. W. Rosenstock, 32°......................1st Deacon
W. Huse Chapman, 32°.................2nd Deacon
Charles H. Sleeper, 32°.................Turcopilier
F. E. Hedrick, 32°....Bearer of the Beausant
C. H. W. Aitkens, 32°........Ber. of the White
                                  Strd.
O. L. Sullivan, 32°....Ber of the Black Strd.
F. W. Towle, 32°.................Lt. of the Guard
M. Weissberg, 32°..............................Sentinel

REGULAR MEETINGS

ANNUAL MEETING

Meets in Masonic Temple, The Escolta, Manila
56

MALCAMPO COUNCIL OF KADOSH, No. 2,—Manila

Owes allegiance to the Supreme Council
A. & A. S. R., Southern Jurisdiction, U. S .A.

OFFICERS

Francis Burton Harrison, 32°........Preceptor,
    Residence: Malacañan Palace
    Phone 29, and 830
José McMicking, 32°....First Sub-Preceptor
Conrado Benitez, 30°..Second Sub-Preceptor
Rafael Palma, 30°.............................Chancellor
Isauro Gabaldon, 32°............................Orator
Enrique P. Brias Roxas, 32°............Almoner
Daniel Morelos......................................Secretary
    c /o Philippine Senate
Catalino Lavadia, 32° Marshal of Ceremonies
Mariano Guerrero, 30°..................Turcopilier
Victoriano R. Onrubia, 30°................Draper
Alfonso Sy Cip, 32°.....................First Deacon
Luciano L. Bernabe, 30°........Second Deacon
Venancio Concepcion, 32°............Beausenifer
Francisco Zamora, 30° Br. of White Standard
Isidro R. Morales, 32°Br. of Black Standard
Juan Atayde y Gruet, 30°....Lt. of the Guard
Oskar Baier, 30°..................................Sentinel
John C. Howe, 32°.............................Organist

REGULAR MEETINGS
Fourth Friday of each month

ANNUAL MEETING

Meets in Masonic Temple, The Escolta, Manila.

GAUTAMA CONSISTORY, No. 1, (31° 32°)—Manila

Owes allegiance to the Supreme Council A. & A. S. R., Southern Jurisdiction, U. S .A.

OFFICERS

Charles Henry Magee, 32°..Master of Kadosh
(absent)
Charles A. Tansill, 32° K.C.C.H............Prior
    Residence: 100 Juan Luna
    Phone: 870
Frederic H. Stevens, 32°K.C.C.H...Preceptor
Chester J. Gerkin, 32°....................Chancellor
Newton C. Comfort 32°..........................Orator
Edwin Emil Elser, 32°.........................Almoner
Warren W. Weston, 32°K.C.C.H.....Registrar
Aziz T. Hashim, 32°.........................Treasurer
William J. G. Whiley, 32°................Prelate
John Frank Brown, 32°Master of Ceremonies
William Andrew Weidman, 32°............Expert
Heinrich W. Gangnuss, 32°..Assistant Expert
Charles Sumner Banks, 32°Standard Bearer
Harvey Albert Bordner, 32°Master of Guard
James McCombs Bury 32°................Sentinel

REGULAR MEETINGS

ANNUAL MEETING

Meets in Masonic Temple, The Escolta, Manila

RIZAL CONSISTORY No. 2, M. R. S. Manila

Owes allegiance to the Supreme Council
A. & A. S. R., Southern Jurisdiction, U. S. A.

OFFICERS

Manuel L. Quezon, 32°....Master of Kadosh
   Residence: 404 Lamayan, Sta. Ana
   Phone: 8
Walter W. Marquardt, 32°.....................Prior
Santiago Barcelona, 32°..................Preceptor
Felipe Buencamino, Jr. 32°............Chancellor
Teodoro M. Kalaw, 32...........................Orator
Enrique P. Brias Roxas, 32°............Almoner
Daniel Morelos......................................Registrar
   c/o Philippine Senate
Omar Malcolm Shuman, 32°............Treasurer
Felipe Barreto, 32°.............................Prelate
Harry Lawrence Noble, 32°............Master of
                            Cerem.
Daniel Morelos, 32°..............................Expert
Pablo Herrera, 32°...........Assistant Expert
Primitivo S. Agustin 32°....Standard Bearer
Isidro R. Morales 32°....Master of the Guard
Marshall H. Burnham, Jr. 32°................Tiler
John C. Howe, 32°.............................Organist

REGULAR MEETINGS
Fourth Friday of each month

ANNUAL MEETING

Meets in Masonic Temple, The Escolta, Manila

MAYON CHAPTER NO. 1, O. E. S.
Manila

Instituted October 29, 1904
Subordinate to General Grand Chapter U.S.A.

OFFICERS

Elizabeth Jane Marshall........Worthy Matron
Christian William Rosenstock Worthy Patron
Nellie Freeman Ottofy.........Associate Matron
Louis Ottofy.................................Secreta.y
    Address: 54 Mabini, Ermita, Manila
       Phone 472. P. O. Box 50
Edith May Darneille........................Treasurer
Hazel Coberly Youngberg...........Conductress
Mary Louisa Aitken....Associate Conductress
Jemima King Shuler...............................Adah
Ada May Rosenstock................................Ruth
Alice Rose Doty....................................Esther
Margarett Stewart Gallin....................Martha
Cora Eleanora Thomas........................Electa
Ray Virginia Harvey, P.W.M...........Marshal
Lyla Tery...Warder
Frank W. Towle..................................Sentinel
J. G. Falkenrath..................................Chaplain
Miriam Reich Hedrick.......................Organist

REGULAR MEETINGS
First and Third Fridays each month,
8.30 p.m.

ANNUAL MEETING
December 6, 1918

Meets in Masonic Temple, The Escolta, Manila

SCOTTISH RITE LYCEUM OF THE PHILIPPINES

(Organized December 29, 1907)

OFFICERS

Austin Craig, 32°.................................Preceptor
Manuel Camus, 32°, K.C.C.H.................Prior
Conrado Benitez, 30°.........................Recorder
    Address: Room 27, University Hall,
        Calle Padre Faura.
    Phone: 922.

The Lyceum conducts courses of Masonic tudy, holds quarterly meetings (in March, June, September and December) and furnishes from its membership speakers, in either English or Spanish, to BLUE Lodges which ask its assistance. These addresses are, of course, without cost, occupy from five to fifteen minutes in delivery and where the lodge is too remote to be reached by a speaker, the manuscript of an address will be mailed to the Lodge secretary.

El Liceo habre clase sobre masoneria, da reuniones cada tres meses durante los meses de Marzo, Junio, Septiembre y Diciembre y provee de Oradores en ingles ó en español á la logia, que los necesiten. Los trabajos de dichos oradores desde luego no se pagan. Los discursos durarón por lo menos de 5 á 15 minutos. Y cuando la logia esta por razon de distancia no puede asistir á estos actos el discurso ó los discursos pronuncialos se enviarán al Secretario de la logia por correo.

RELIEF

PHILIPPINE MASONIC BOARD O[
RELIEF, P. O. Box 598, Manila.

The objects of this Board are to exter
relief to all worthy sojourning members
the Masonic Fraternity, their widows an
orphans and members of their families, wh
may be in distress, and to advance the tru
principles of Masonry in the Philippine I
lands. The Board is composed of the Wo
shipful Master, Senior Warden, Junior Wa
den, Secretary, and Treasurer of each
the lodges contributing to its funds.

Edwin   E.   Elser..............................Secretar
        Kneedler Building
        Phones: 129 and 437

ı

٠

Meets at time and place designated by
President.

72

NILE SHRINERS ASSOCIATION OF THE PHILIPPINE ISLANDS

Subordinate to and under the jurisdiction of Nile Temple, Ancient Arabic Order of the Nobles of the Mystic Shrine.

Organized January 5, 1916.

Composed of members of Nile Temple reated in the Philippine Islands Jan. 31, 914 and April 8, 1916. Organized to pro- iote the interests of the Mystic Shrine and f Nile Temple and its members in the 'hilippine Islands.

OFFICERS

Toble William F. Gallin, Jr., ...President
Toble Walter R. Macfarlane, Vice President
Toble Edwin E. Elser......................Treasurer
Toble W. Huse Chapman, ...Secretary

(Masonic Temple, Escolta)

The above officers with Nobles Stanton Toungberg, and E. W. Wilbur compose the Ixecutive committee.

Ieets at the call of the Executive committee

Next Ceremonial in Manila will be held !uring 1918.

"Aleikum es Salaam"

MASONIC TEMPLE ASSOCIATION INCORPORATED.

P. O. Box 398.   Phone 1505.

BOARD OF DIRECTORS.

Milton E. Springer.............................Presiden
    35-41 Plaza Sta. Cruz
    Phone: 2033.
C. M. Cotterman.........................Vice-Presiden
W. Huse Chapman............................Secretar
    Room 321, Masonic Temple
    Phone: 1505
C. H. Sleeper...................................Treasure
E. J. Westerhouse.............................Directo
E. E. Elser.......................................Directo
C. M. Colton....................................Directo
W. W. Weston...................................Directo
Tomas Earnshaw.................................Directo
J. F. Bromfield.................................Directo
G. W. Mayo......................................Directo
F. E. Hedrick...................................Directo

BOARD MEETINGS
First Monday each month

ANNUAL MEETING
Fourth Monday in January

Meets in Masonic Temple, The Escolta, Manil

THE FAR EASTERN FREEMASON

(El Francmason del Extremo Oriente)

A monthly magazine devoted to the interests of the Craft and primarily of the Scottish Rite in the Extreme Orient.

Published under the auspices of the
JOINT ADMINISTRATIVE COUNCIL
of the
SCOTTISH RITE BODIES OF THE
VALLEY OF MANILA

Publication Committee:
Frederic H. Stevens, 32, K.C.C.H., chairman; H. Lawrence Noble, 32; Teodoro M. Kalaw, 32.
Staff:
H. Lawrence Noble, Editor of the English Section.
John F. Brown, Assistant Editor of the English Section.
Teodore M. Kalaw, Director, Sección Castellana.
Leo Fischer, Assistant Director, Sección Castellana.
Manuel X. Burgos, Jr., Assistant Director, Sección Castellana.
Frederic H. Stevens, Administrador.

Subscription rates: ₱3.00 (Philippine currency) per annum; $2.00 (United States currency) to the United States and foreign countries.
Address: The Far Eastern Freemason, P. O. Box 1335, Manila, P. I.

MASONIC SOJOURNERS' ASSOCIA. TION

P. O. Box 687, Manila

Organized October 13, 1907.

At the annual meeting in October, 1917, the association was dissolved, the purpose of the association having been accomplished.

The funds of the Association amounting to slightly more than ₱2,000.00 were deposited with the Secretary of the Manila Bodies of the Scottish Rite as the nucleus of a fund to be raised for the establshment of a Masonic Widows and Orphan House in the Philippines.

The seal of the association was presented to the Most Worshipful Grand Lodge of the Philippine Islands.

H. E. Heacock Co.

Wholesale and Retail Jewelers

MAKERS OF
ARTISTIC and DISTINCTIVE
MASONIC JEWELRY

Special Order Work
Executed by Master Craftsmen

The Store of Quality

H. E. HEACOCK Co.

Heacock Bldg.   121-133 Escolta

Correspondence regarding the 1919 Edition of this Directory should be addressed to Chas. M. Colton, Masonic Temple, Manila, P. I.

www.ingramcontent.com/pod-product-compliance
Lightning Source LLC
Chambersburg PA
CBHW032119280326
41933CB00009B/914